ALEXANDER GRAHAM BELL

DISCOVER THE LIFE OF AN INVENTOR

Ann Gaines

Rourke Publishing LLC
Vero Beach, Florida 32964

www.rourkepublishing.com

PHOTO CREDITS:
© Archive Photo, Library of Congress

EDITORIAL SERVICES:
Pamela Schroeder

Library of Congress Cataloging-in-Publication Data

Gaines, Ann.
    Alexander Graham Bell / Ann Gaines
        p. cm. — (Discover the life of an inventor)
    Includes bibliographical references and index.
    ISBN 1-58952-117-X
    1. Bell, Alexander Graham, 1847-1922—Juvenile literature. 2.
    Inventors—United States—Biography—Juvenile literature. 3.
Telephone—   History—
Juvenile literature. [1. Bell, Alexander Graham, 1947-1922. 2.
Inventors.] I. Title.

TK6143.B4 G35 2001
621.385'092—dc21
[B]   2001019376

Printed in the USA

TABLE OF CONTENTS

ALEXANDER GRAHAM BELL
AND HIS INVENTIONS

Alexander Graham Bell tried to invent things to help people. His best idea was the phone. He thought it would help the deaf hear. Now his phone helps all people talk to each other.

He had many more ideas. One invention was the **iron lung**. It helped people breathe who could not breathe on their own.

Alexander Graham Bell shows off his phone.

ALEXANDER GRAHAM BELL GROWS UP

Alexander Graham Bell was born on March 3, 1847, in Edinburgh, Scotland. He was the second son of Alexander and Eliza Bell. His mother taught him at home.

As a young man, he became a speech teacher like his father and grandfather. He moved to the United States in 1871. He found a job at the Boston School for the Deaf in Massachusetts.

Alexander's grandfather was a speech teacher.

DEAFNESS, SOUND, AND ELECTRIC CURRENT

During the day, Alexander taught deaf children. At night he worked to make a machine to send human voices over a wire.

He remembered talking to his deaf grandmother. He always put his mouth near her forehead. Then he would speak to her in a slow voice. He had learned that speech was a force that traveled through the air.

Alexander was a teacher by the age of 15.

Alexander's idea was to turn human sounds into electric **current**. He would send the electric current over a wire. Another machine would receive it. Then that machine would turn the current back into sound.

Beginning in 1874, he worked with Thomas Watson to build the machines. They were a good team. Thomas Watson was a skilled builder. Alexander Graham Bell understood sound and electric current.

Thomas Watson became Bell's good friend.

THE ELECTRIC SPEECH MACHINE

On July 26, 1874, Alexander figured out how to build his machine. He called it his electric speech machine. Today, people call it a telephone.

The electric speech machine was really two machines. The machine to turn sound into electric current was called the **transmitter**. The machine to turn the electric current back into sound was called the **receiver**.

Alexander Graham Bell is best know for his invention of the telephone.

Alexander and Tom Watson worked to build the electric speech machine. On June 3, 1875, Alexander and Tom had success! They transmitted speech sounds.

On March 12, 1876, Alexander tested his newest machine. He spoke into the transmitter. "Mr. Watson, come here. I want to see you." Tom Watson listened on the receiver. He heard Alexander! They had made a phone.

The first working transmitter used by Bell

SUCCESS!

In June, 1876, Alexander brought his phone to the **Centennial Exhibition** in Philadelphia. He showed people how it worked. In August, 1876, Alexander made a telephone call to another house more than 5 miles (8 kilometers) away.

By 1884, long distance calls could be made between Boston and New York City. Phones were used in homes and offices in the United States and around the world.

Alexander showed his phone to hundreds of people.

AN INVENTOR'S LIFE

Alexander kept inventing. He made a new type of phone. It could transmit words on a beam of light. He was interested in flying machines. He built large kites and gliders. At age 75, he invented a **hydrofoil** boat. It was the fastest boat in the world at that time.

He kept working, but had time to enjoy his farm. He lived in a large family home in Nova Scotia.

Alexander liked to build kites.

REMEMBERING ALEXANDER GRAHAM BELL

When Alexander Graham Bell died at his home on August 2, 1922, he was world famous. As a **tribute**, all telephone service in the United States stopped for 1 minute.

The **Library of Congress** now owns many of Alexander's letters, notes, and drawings of his inventions. Visitors to the Smithsonian Institution in Washington, D.C., can learn all about him.

During his final years, Alexander put many of his ideas on paper.

IMPORTANT DATES TO REMEMBER

1847	Born in Edinburgh, Scotland (March 3)
1871	Moved to the United States
1874	Began working with Thomas Watson
1874	Figured out how to make a phone
1875	Transmitted speech sounds by phone
1876	Public first saw phone
1876	Phone call between houses 5 miles from each other
1922	Died in Nova Scotia (August 2)

GLOSSARY

Centennial Exhibition (sen TEN ee el ek se BISH en) — a world's fair held to celebrate the independence of the United States

current (KUR ent) — flow of electricity through a wire

hydrofoil (HY dreh foyl) — a winglike piece attached to the front of a boat that raises the boat out of the water

iron lung (EYE ern LUNG) — an airtight metal tank that surrounds the body but not the head; it forces the lungs to breathe

Library of Congress (LY brer ee UHV KAHN gress) — the nation's library, located in Washington, D.C.

receiver (reh SEE ver) — a machine that gets messages

transmitter (trans MIT er) — a machine that sends messages

tribute (TRIB yoot) — way to honor a person

INDEX

Further Reading

Gearheart, Sarah. *The Telephone*. Atheneum, 1999.

Websites To Visit

http://tntn.essortment.com/biographyalexand_rfx.htm
www.pbs.org/wgbh/amex/telephone

About The Author

Ann Gaines is the author of many children's nonfiction books. She has also worked as a researcher in the American Civilization Program at the University of Texas.